BEYOND BELIEFS

The Lost Teachings of
Sydney Banks

BY LINDA QUIRING

CCB Publishing
British Columbia, Canada

Beyond Beliefs:
The Lost Teachings of Sydney Banks

Copyright ©2016 by Linda Quiring
ISBN-13   978-1-77143-260-3
First Edition

Library and Archives Canada Cataloguing in Publication
Quiring, Linda, 1944-, author
Beyond beliefs : the lost teachings of Sydney Banks
/ by Linda Quiring. -- First edition.
Issued in print and electronic formats.
ISBN 978-1-77143-260-3 (pbk.).--ISBN 978-1-77143-261-0 (pdf)
Additional cataloguing data available from Library and Archives
Canada

Cover artwork credit:
Photo by Michael Levy – Flat Earth Photography
Website: http://flatearthphoto.com
Facebook: https://www.facebook.com/WestCoastWonders

Publisher: CCB Publishing
              British Columbia, Canada
              www.ccbpublishing.com

DEDICATION

I would like to dedicate this book to those who made it happen! Firstly...

Jack Pransky, who learned of the 1979 manuscript of *Beyond Beliefs* and would not rest until it saw the light of day.

Jack convinced Paul Rabinovitch, my publisher, to take a chance on an unknown author and publish these very early writings of Sydney Banks.

Always, to Sydney Banks, a simple, ordinary man who vowed to change the world with his startling message, and did!

BEYOND BELIEFS

There I was, at Christian McNeill's house in Glasgow, Scotland on my 2014 Three Principles European Tour, as she handed a book to me across the table.

"Have you seen this?" she asked.

It was an original copy of *Island of Knowledge*, given to her by its author, Linda Quiring. Christian had recently come back from a visit to Salt Spring Island.

"No, what is it?"

"It's the first book ever written about Syd Banks."

"You're kidding! What?!"

I had only been involved with the Three Principles for twenty-three years. How could I have never heard of the first book about Sydney Banks, especially since the words in it attributed to Syd were his own? I couldn't believe my eyes and ears.

I flipped it open. Wow! This was incredible stuff! A true lost treasure, found.

"Who is Linda Quiring?"

"She's the first person ever to be helped by Syd."

"Not the woman who, rumor has it, was released from a mental institution and told she needed to be on medication and get periodic shock treatments for the rest of her life, but after talking with Syd didn't need any of that?"

"The very same."

I was flabbergasted. Before I left Christian's house I gobbled down the entire book. I thought it was the best Sydney Banks book I had ever read. I couldn't believe it had been hidden from me and I guessed from most everyone who had found Syd and the Three Principles understanding around the time I did and since.

I needed to get hold of a copy of this book. I tracked down Linda.

At first Linda seemed a bit wary of me, but after talking some I think she saw my motivations were pure. This led to a few long telephone conversations where she regaled me with fascinating stories of the history of the early Salt Spring Island days as she remembered it, something I had always been fascinated by but knew little about.

After we developed excellent rapport I suggested if she wanted to reprint this book I'd bet my publisher would love to republish it. Linda became intrigued. I was a little nervous about its hippie overtones, but after all this was the mid-1970s. To me this was a beautiful historical document of the way it all began. Plus it was closest to Syd's raw, unfiltered enlightenment experience than anything Syd had previously written or audiotaped.

Somewhere in the midst of these conversations Linda dropped this line on me: "And I have another book that Syd and I wrote together, but we had a falling out at the time so it has never seen the light of day. Apparently not many people knew that Syd and

I made amends and continued to be friends for the rest of his life, but the book has been sitting there ever since. It's called, *Beyond Beliefs*..."

Whoa!

"This has to come out!" I thought. Linda told me this book was written just as the "psychologists" started coming over to the Island, just as things began to change, just as Syd began to realize his message needed to be put out more professionally, just as, perhaps, some of the feeling on the Island started to change a bit.

Linda realized she needed to blow dust off the copy sitting somewhere on her shelf — she was sure she had it somewhere — and she became excited about the idea of this book actually being published. Again my publisher jumped at the chance. We figured the reprint of *Island of Knowledge* had to come first, so we worked to bring that to fruition. Then it was time for *Beyond Beliefs*.

Recently, I came upon this direct quote from Syd on a very early tape, in which he states:

"The other night in our house we were working on Linda's second book, and there was about 28 people in the house at the time, and it was really beautiful — beautiful night, much hilarity, really [unintelligible word]. And Linda's growth in the book from the beginning — she wrote a book called *Island of Knowledge*, and what it was was an encounter with me from the first day she met me until now — and I'd really advise, if you want to read a nice book, you should read it, because

every page in that book has the secret you're looking for. Every single page. My wife and I were
talking the other night, looking back when we
first met Bill and Linda—this is the parts out of
the book: how they've changed, how it's come to
life, how they found life. And it was all so simple,
because you don't have to go anyplace to find it.
It's inside. Just go back inside and find that
truth…"

--from the tape labeled "Early Syd" (undated),
by way of Christian McNeill from Allan
Flood's private collection

I cannot tell you what an honor and privilege it
has been for me to take Syd's original words that no
one but Linda had ever seen and work as editor to
help this book come to be. Linda is such a wonderful
writer and Syd's voice rang out so clearly that very
little editing was needed. Now I am exceptionally
happy to help share this book with the rest of the
world. Speaking personally, I found gems galore
within it, especially later in the book as it unfolds.

Thank you, Linda, for sharing this awesome gift
with us. I, personally, am indebted to you…

Jack Pransky
Boca Raton, Florida
November, 2015

In early 1979, five years after Sydney Banks and I began working and writing together, we completed the manuscript of our next book, *Beyond Beliefs*. Our first book, *Island of Knowledge*, had sold 2,000 copies, but a time of dramatic change was upon us.

Syd had gathered around him dozens of students eager to hear him speak and learn from his amazing experience. Syd was truly passionate about sharing his wisdom and spoke to anyone interested whether from a religious organization, teachers or educators, and finally, the therapists and psychologists who began to arrive on Salt Spring Island, in particular Dr. Roger Mills.

Syd was soon travelling constantly, from Eugene, Oregon to San Francisco, Los Angeles, Minnesota and Florida where centers were organized to share his teachings. Our time of working and writing together came to an end as the wider world called him, and we would never again work together, although we remained friends until his passing in 2009.

It soon became apparent to Syd and others that psychology was the way his teachings could spread and ultimately benefit the most people. As our paths diverged I was called to the spiritual path Syd had guided me along, and I had little interest in psychology, as I felt it had failed me when I most needed help before meeting Sydney Banks.

Syd and I continued our relationship and met several times a year to discuss our lives, families and experiences, and although I attended one or two large gatherings where he spoke I never became a student of the Three Principles that the message had evolved into. Somehow, the lone copy of this manuscript I had typed on an old Selectric typewriter gathered dust on a bookshelf for almost 35 years.

Enter Jack Pransky, a teacher of the Three Principles for 23 years! One day the phone rang, Jack introduced himself and inquired about *Island of Knowledge* and we spoke at length several times. One day, I dropped the bombshell that a second manuscript existed, and Jack would not rest until his vision came to pass; to my great delight, that *Island of Knowledge* would be reprinted and *Beyond Beliefs* finally come to light, because he believed Syd's words would be helpful to so many people.

Life is sometimes stranger than fiction, and it now seems as though destiny preserved that lone copy, resting perhaps until the world was ready for the incredibly direct and intuitive message of that 'raw, unfiltered enlightenment experience.'

And to my teacher and friend, Sydney Banks, what an amazing journey we travelled together and apart. Thank you.

Linda Quiring
Salt Spring Island, British Columbia
November 11th, 2015

Photo of Sydney Banks walking Linda Quiring
down the aisle at her wedding, 1976.

CHAPTER 1

IT'S ALL INSIDE

Salt Spring is an island of magic. Each season brings with it dramatic change.

Now in springtime I can almost feel the earth stirring, preparing herself for new growth, for a new cycle of life.

Bill and I drove down the familiar country road. The early evening air held just a hint of warmth but seemed to promise more. I felt excited, strangely exhilarated but perhaps it was only the coming of spring.

It was an evening filled with magic and poetry and we looked forward eagerly to the coming hours. Bill and I were on our way to Syd and Barb's where together we would share a journey as we had countless times before.

We were adventurers and our journey led within, where the true secrets of life lie. We had taken that first step and found before us a world fresh and new. We had begun hesitantly. Now, we knew we had found the way. It did not matter that some did not accompany us for there were many who did.

A man lives in our midst, a man of extreme ordinariness. He had shown us the way.

With mere words, words so familiar yet totally enigmatic he had shown us a world beyond the veils of illusion. He had read few books but spoke knowingly of the secrets of life.

The words were always simple; the impact profound.

Bill turned down the long winding driveway and inside the house we found a room that seemed to glow. We often spoke of this room, of its special quality. Here, it seemed, our lives had really begun.

With warmth and vibrant color the living room beckons, yet the mood is soft, subtle. The décor is neither old-fashioned nor modern but a blend of both. The effect is one of timelessness.

Before the window, the sea; a constant ebb and flow and always from the hearth a fire welcomes. "Come in," the room says. "Find a comfortable spot. Have a cup of tea and be at home."

That's exactly what we did.

Almost at once the telephone rang and Syd was soon speaking with the greatest of enthusiasm.

"Find the secret of your inner states of consciousness and this world you know will not be a belief, it will be a FACT!"

Bill and I glanced at each other. I felt a little guilty about eavesdropping but this conversation was fascinating!

"It is FACTS, or KNOWING which unveil the simplicity of life. It is this KNOWING that rids you of the petty beliefs that create unhappiness and sickness of mind. Knowing brings love and understanding beyond your wildest imagination!"

Such a statement was very typical of Syd and always brought puzzled looks. The words would seem to make no sense whatsoever. Yet we knew these same words had the power to bring to the listener the true knowledge of life.

I had learned it was impossible to figure out the meaning of Syd's words. We must listen and accept with faith that understanding would come. And it came, not with intellectual activity but in quiet, peaceful moments through an experience of hearing or seeing truth.

I recalled the first time I had heard such words. I'd asked Syd what he meant by HEARING and SEEING.

"It cannot be told," he said.

"It is an EXPERIENCE of seeing the world with greater clarity. Not only your world but also the world which lies within."

Well, this had certainly been news to me! I hadn't known what a state of consciousness was, and if I had one I felt it was far from perfect. Yet something in his words had opened a door to a place inside, a place dimly remembered.

Eventually Syd returned from the telephone, a smile on his face.

"He's just like you," he said. "He thinks too

much!"

At one time I would have bristled, jumped up and militantly demanded, "What do you mean by that?"

Now, I knew what he meant! The benefits of having a guide; one who had gone before, time; experience; all had shown me. The only obstacle to my happiness, peace of mind, the wisdom I sought, was and always had been... my own mind!

Syd went over to his favourite chair. Barb brought in tea and cookies and we talked. Our conversation as usual went here and there, from gardening to awareness, to Bill's new shirt and always back to awareness.

The only reminder of the hours passing came from the clock which chimed the hours and the half. We soon forgot all thoughts of everyday reality as Syd spoke to us of the life within, the only REAL life. Often the words went beyond our comprehension.

As he spoke, Syd's voice became softer and the words more powerful. He seemed to be speaking from far away, describing to us a world we had never visited. His eyes were alive and sparkling, his face totally at peace. I have never seen such a look on any other human being. A moment came full of such intensity it seemed we might almost grasp that world of which he spoke.

Then, Syd smiles! A great, huge, grinning smile. His face, his whole being seems to light up and though I've seen it a thousand times, it is always a delight!

Part of it is pure joy, the joy of simply being alive. Part of it seems to say this whole thing is just one big cosmic joke, too indescribably funny for words. Part of the smile is love, just love.

Syd continued to speak, looking directly at me. I felt somehow that the words came not from him, from Syd, but from a place beyond.

"All life is energy manifest into form via thought. The source of this energy contains the knowledge all mankind seeks. Here lies the secret of the self. Here, my dear Linda, lies the secret of life!"

The words were compelling. Once again they assured me there was nothing I could or need do, for the knowledge I sought already lie deep within.

The clock chimed, telling us it was time to leave and we said good-night to Syd and Barb. How fortunate we were to have such friends!

Bill and I drove along in silence, enjoying a quiet moment. Suddenly Bill spoke, his voice full of excitement.

"It's amazing," he said. "It's just amazing!"

"What is?" I asked.

"It's Syd! He's got it! He's really got the secret! And he found it in one second. Unbelievable!"

"I know what you mean," I said. "When I hear him speak, I know, I just KNOW he speaks truth. Yet when I think about it, my mind comes in and says, "That's impossible. How can anyone find the answer in one SECOND? You have to study for years or read a thousand books no one can understand. You think, "It just can't be that simple!"

"But it really is," said Bill, "The mind just won't accept the fact!"

We both laughed. It had been a perfect evening.

CHAPTER 2

THE FACTS OF LIFE

The next morning Bill went off to work and I spent the day puttering around the house. It was a gift to spend the day alone, doing all the little things I like to do. I watered my plants, dusted and started in on the dishes.

I had a beautiful, warm feeling inside and it felt good to be me. I looked up through the window where sun poured in, through the trees to the meadow beyond.

"I'm so lucky," I thought. "I have everything I've ever wanted.

"It's true!" I realized.

"I do have everything. A wonderful husband, a fine son, countless friends."

Joy surged from within and tears came to my eyes. Then the picture of me by the sink, crying in the dishwater was too funny. I laughed aloud, feeling totally free, totally happy.

Years before, living in sickness and despair I would never have dreamed such a feeling possible. All I had done was listen to a man speak the truth about life and I had been given life.

That evening after Gary was asleep I asked Bill if

he'd like some fresh air. We walked in the moonlight down to the canal as we had so many times in the past three years. Our walk is always a special time, sharing an hour together after a full day. At the little bridge we stopped to talk for a few moments before going back up the hill and home.

"You know," I said, "I've been thinking about Syd and what he said last night. About facts."

"What about it?" asked Bill.

"Well," I began, "he mentioned facts on the telephone. To me, a fact is a fact. Like two plus two equals four. But when Syd says fact I know it means something different."

"Why don't you ask him about it," suggested Bill.

"I think I just might do that!"

The next time we visited I had my question ready: "Syd, what is fact?"

Syd turned from where he had been gazing out the window, looked at me intently for a moment and then sat down.

"How can the mind possibly comprehend a fact when you insist on living in your mind of beliefs?

"My friend, a FACT cannot be explained, only experienced. KNOWING is a fact! SEEING is a fact! Each new level of consciousness brings FACT!

"You see, the mind of man can only understand a belief. The universal mind deals not with beliefs, but with FACTS. The mind of man cannot possibly understand a fact for the mind of man itself is only a belief, NOT a fact!"

I sat quite speechless. I realized I had come with a preconceived idea about fact; a belief. Syd would answer my question, explain all about fact. I would understand completely, say, "Yeah, right!" and that would be that.

But his words went far beyond intellectual understanding. I felt my ego had just been put in its place!

"It's that old ego again," I chuckled.

Syd smiled and went on. "It is the ego that stops us from finding what we seek. It is an image of self-importance laden with fear and insecurity. It is man's worst enemy!"

"I thought man was his own worst enemy," said Bill.

Syd snapped his fingers. "Exactly!"

He rose and walked across the room towards the television set. For half an hour we watched Archie Bunker stumble hilariously through the game of life. I had completely forgotten about facts.

A little later, Syd began again to speak.

"Imagine," he said. "I was forty-three years old and had never known a fact. The first time I HEARD a fact it was so overwhelming I could hardly stand the beauty. The beauty that came to me with the realization of this fact was so fascinating I never slept for three days and three nights.

"On the third night I was full to overflowing with love. Without warning my chariot arrived. I was home in the land of knowledge. I was free.

"Indeed, it was true. All the secrets of life lie within our own conscious state."

A hush followed Syd's words, a deep and peaceful silence. I had heard him speak often of his experience but never before had he told of it so movingly. His eyes literally shone with an unutterable love.

With each of us he had shared that love. I felt honored that in my lifetime I had known such a man.

As if bewildered by such powerful emotion, my thoughts returned. Syd had mentioned a chariot and his words evoked a beautiful picture in my mind. A golden chariot, led by gallant white stallions coming and in a moment whisking us away to the Land of Knowledge. How incredible!

"Tell us more about this chariot, Syd."

"The second you are ready, the chariot will appear and shine so brightly with the Light of Knowledge that it shows the way home."

Bill then asked, "Can this chariot be recognized only by people who see facts?"

"Yes," Syd replied, "this is true. Sometimes people build chariots from beliefs instead of facts. Then the chariot, like the beliefs that built it, turn out to be illusions and of no value.

"A belief chariot will take you through paths filled with pit holes and darkness. You see, such a chariot has no light and must always become lost.

"A chariot created from facts is a powerful thing. It is so full of love and understanding, the mind of man cannot comprehend it.

"If you ever encounter this beautiful vehicle and recognize the light of love which shines from it, you are truly lucky. The beauty is that this chariot is available at will to any living soul. Believe me, when you are ready your chariot will appear."

Syd spoke so convincingly and so confidently, I began to feel my chariot might arrive any minute. I basked in this feeling of confidence for a moment. I was quite pleased with myself.

"However," Syd warned, "if you don't recognize it and attach it with beliefs to stop its progress, then you are a fool and the price is costly."

Oh, oh. My confidence wavered. I had the feeling Syd could read my mind. Each time I thought I knew something, I'd find there was so much more to learn. I was just beginning.

"Syd. I just don't understand."

"What I have just said is quite unexplainable! Yet by listening to the unexplainable you may experience a FACT!"

Syd smiled. He had that inscrutable look on his face.

"A mind belief," he said, "is like a pop-gun without a POP!"

We burst into laughter. We never really knew what he was going to say next. But I was still puzzled. I really wanted to get this.

"Is knowledge the chariot?" I asked.

"Knowledge," replied Syd, "creates the readiness to SEE the chariot. In actual fact, the chariot is not the knowledge, but THE WAY. THE WAY is non-tangible. It cannot be expressed in words. One must go beyond the words, to find the experience."

We talked for a few minutes more and then Bill mentioned the light Syd had spoken of. It was interesting, for the Bible, many religious and sacred teachings also spoke of 'light'.

I asked, "What kind of light does the chariot have?"

"To all humans who SEE this chariot, it shines with the light of hope guiding others to heaven here on earth.

"There is only one golden chariot. There are many made of tinsel and threads which fall apart at the slightest touch. When you are ready I guarantee it will appear and guide you home. Home is where the secret of thought and its relationship to life lies.

"ALL LIFE IS THOUGHT, and THAT, my dear friends, is a FACT!"

Suddenly Syd sat erect in his chair.

"I think we have spoken enough of the chariot. I can see your old minds are thinking again. Stop trying to figure it out and just listen."

He shook his head as if to testify that it was quite useless.

"Just listen," he said. "It will all happen."

His words took me back to the day years before when Bill and I first spoke with Syd. Two lost, frightened and confused people, we had understood nothing of the way of life he spoke of.

"Just listen," he had said. "It will all happen."

His words had given us hope then, and today we had not only hope, we'd gained an unconquerable faith in the future.

His words had come true!

Beyond Beliefs

CHAPTER 3

TWO DIFFERENT WORLDS

We are learning to live inside, in the heart. I know now that we do not find love but that we must uncover the love that already lies hidden beneath the maze of our thoughts.

Tomorrow, I may again be tricked by my mind into living in the illusion, but the illusion grows weaker. It has lost its power. The new reality has become a solid strength, always within me. It is me!

I did not always live in such a reality, for until I heard truth my world was quite different. I can remember a time, though I seldom do, when life held no joy, no hope. The world was grey, lifeless; the way I felt, the way I was...

My childhood had been rich with dreams of an exciting life. A charming prince would carry me away, we would live in a cottage by the sea, happily ever after. But that was a fairy tale. I learned it had nothing to do with reality.

All too soon, I grew up and life meant hard work, illness. It meant a first marriage that ended in failure. A small son had come into my life and bound his life to mine. I clung to him in my loneliness and hoped his life would be different, but I could share with him only my fear and confusion. I wanted to control him, and he, with the innate wisdom of a child, rebelled.

I became ill and old before my time. I was hospitalized with heart problems and feared I might die. I was then twenty-three years old. My kidneys were failing rapidly and I was allergic to almost everything.

I suffered constant headaches and began to wear glasses. The time came when I felt with certainty that there was nothing to live for. I actually prayed I might die for I was too afraid to take my own life, a life that had become unbearable.

Yet I knew I must carry on and take care of my son. So, in desperation I pulled myself out of this lethargy and began to search. I searched, not for happiness, for I no longer believed in it, but for some kind of 'answer.'

My search led first to books. There I found some answers. The great thinkers had great ideas but the words to me were just words. I exchanged a few beliefs for newer ones, but I did not feel any different.

Soon I learned of 'awareness,' of people who were doing something about life. I found and joined an 'awareness' group and for the first time in years I felt a ray of hope.

The group was exciting, I'll say that much for it. I spent six months beating pillows with a 'hate stick.' This, they assured me, would get rid of hate. We pushed each other around. This would rid us of hostility. We cried and screamed. Screaming, it appeared, was a great method of therapy; it got rid of almost anything. I learned to 'express my feelings' and found the only thing I got rid of were my friends.

The glimmer of hope I'd felt in the beginning faded. It became boring, repetitious and my heart just wasn't in it. Amid cries of 'chicken' from my fellow groupies I finally hung up my hate stick for good.

Besides, something more important was happening. I had met Bill at the group and we'd fallen madly in love. For a time the world was bright again for I believed that 'Love Conquers All.'

It might have, but at the group we had both learned of Freedom. Freedom meant being your own person, doing your own thing. It was all very nice in theory but did not work very well in fact. This was the '70's, after all.

We believed in 'open marriage.' We felt traditional marriage was outmoded, a thing of the past. It had no place in today's society.

And so we lived together, worlds apart. I felt I truly loved Bill and that he loved me, yet our relationship was filled with conflict, jealousy and insecurity. How often we quarreled and separated!

The only thing we really shared was a desire to find ourselves. Together we travelled through a maze of trips, teachers, methods and books.

We tried yoga. My posture improved; it was a beautiful exercise. But it did not bring peace.

We tried meditation. It brought a welcome hour of relaxation but it did not bring knowledge.

We tried diets, health food. We did breathing exercises. We read scores of books. Each told of a sure way to find happiness. But we did not find it.

Finally we hit upon the solution! We would move to the country, go 'back to the land.' Here we would live a quiet, simple life. Far from pollution, noise and traffic we would grow our own food, we would find real freedom.

How innocent we were!

We completely changed the way we lived, dressed, and talked. We changed our whole way of life, but we did not change. Within months the grand dream evaporated like mist under a burning sun.

Bill and I separated bitterly and I retreated into a world of sedation. For a year I had been under psychiatric care and had been given increasing amounts of medication. Now, even the twenty or so tranquillizers and anti-depressants I took each day could not still the blind panic, the continual fear.

I awoke one day in a mental hospital. I had finally done it! I'd gone crazy! I was having shock treatments. They gave me the maximum number although I felt five or six would have been adequate. Then they sent me home. The prognosis was not very hopeful.

"You have suffered a trauma, possibly in early childhood. You will need many years of analysis. You will be on medication for the rest of your life. You will need to return for more shock therapy regularly."

Two weeks later, I learned of a man on Salt Spring Island who wished to share with others what he'd learned about life. His name was Sydney Banks.

Almost three years have passed since the day I wandered, unaware, into the presence of truth. That day, I first heard truth.

Immediately the knowledge I'd gained began to manifest in my life. Bill and I had reunited. We still had problems but they faded quickly beneath the light of our new understanding. After two short weeks I threw away all of my medication and have never wanted or needed them since.

My health changed and I became vibrant, happy. There was no room in my life for illness.

I walked away from the past as surely and confidently as if it had never been.

I had heard truth. A few short words changed my destiny. Syd and Barb had a quality about them I had never experienced. They were calm, they were secure. I felt that quality as surely as I have ever felt anything.

It was strength, as solid and tangible as this pen in my hand. The words they told me did not make sense. It didn't matter.

That day, I knew in my heart I had been touched by something so vast and wonderful it could not be put into words. I had been touched by Life. The long search was over and the dreams of childhood had now become my reality.

Beyond Beliefs

CHAPTER 4

IT JUST IS!

The days turned to months, months flowed into years. Our dream has not become dull and tarnished with age; rather it shines for us with increasing brightness.

Once I listened as Syd spoke to a small group of people. In the midst of a sentence he paused and said, "You see, there's a flow to life…" He went on, but I heard little else. His words had touched me with their powerful simplicity. For a moment I had been that flow.

I felt within the joy of surrender, of accepting life as it comes, of going wherever it might lead.

I learned to flow with life, up and down, back and forth, but always moving, growing, experiencing. I learned to see levels of consciousness and I see my own levels rise and fall unceasingly.

I learned of free will, that in every moment I can make the choice for happiness or for unhappiness. With the knowledge of each new experience I learned to make the choice for happiness.

A warm day in April found us again at Syd and Barb's home. We'd been invited to spend these hours with them and we felt it both an honor and a gift. The four of us sat, surrounded by a huge expanse of lawn.

Near the house, the little bronze mermaid serenely knelt and forever emptied her bowl into the fountain. The constant trickle of water lulled the senses and we became as serene as she.

The afternoon slipped away and never had I enjoyed the warmth of spring so early and so leisurely. Towards evening the sound of waves slapping against the shore lured us down to the sea.

The moon was rising from behind a far island, flaming with the last colors of the sun still upon it. We found a log half-buried in the damp sand and sat together for a quiet timeless moment.

A slight movement brought my thoughts back from where they had been drifting between sea and sky, and I saw the moon was now high. All thoughts and cares of the world vanished. In such moments I had experienced my deepest understanding of life. I felt with a warm and glowing peace the fullness of life itself.

"How different the world is," I said, "when we begin to see it."

I could never have believed such a world existed, yet now I am surrounded by it. I know it has always been here but I couldn't see it. The world has become so exciting and mysterious. You want to go up to people and say, "Look!" but you know they can't see it either. At least not until they're ready.

"Syd," I laughed, "you used to talk about SEEING. I thought it was a trick.

"That you just snapped your eyeballs into a

certain position or something, and then you SAW!

"Now, I just see. I see what's been here all along."

I had become quite enthused by now and saw that Syd was smiling.

"Please," I asked, "tell us more about SEEING."

"SEEING," he began, "leads to KNOWING. On the other hand, KNOWING is SEEING all the time."

For a second I felt my thoughts scurry forward to analyze this rather challenging statement.

"KNOWING," he continued, "is absolutely unexplainable. One could say, "IT JUST IS!""

"But, but..." I thought. My thoughts became somewhat frayed at the edges. They were certainly no match for an absolute, definite, IT JUST IS!

"Ah," I thought, "the futility of the intellect when confronted by wisdom."

Syd went on, quite casually, as if the meaning of his words were quite obvious, although IT JUST IS was a little too deep for me.

"Can you explain what you mean by that, Syd?" I asked.

"Just is," he said, "is SEEING what-is instead of what-isn't."

I was almost afraid to ask the next question. He had lost me and I felt any further questioning would mystify me even more. But Syd had a gift of making one extremely curious. I plunged ahead anyway, knowing my next question made no sense whatever.

"Syd, what is 'what-isn't?'"

"What-isn't is what the mind sees of what-is. What-is is life in perfect motion."

His words left no impression whatsoever on my mind, which by now was quite blank. Something told me his answer made about as much sense as my question, yet somehow it all seemed perfectly reasonable.

Always, during these conversations the point came where mind just called it a day, tucked itself in, and said, "Good night!"

Syd, however, continued as if the frivolities of the mind were of no consequence.

"What-is appears when mind transcends itself to a higher level of consciousness. This same state is known as a state of meditation."

"You know," said Bill, "when I used to meditate I thought it would bring knowledge. Now I find it's the other way around. It is true knowledge that brings the feeling of a calm and open mind."

"Right!" exclaimed Syd. "People confuse 'meditation' with the 'state of meditation.' One is an outside belief. The other is a fact. The state of meditation is a level of consciousness unknown to the mind. It is a separate reality. It is a conscious space where all the answers you seek lie.

"Find the knowledge that lies within. Here you will find your state of meditation. The 'act of meditation' soothes the mind on your journey through life.

The 'state of meditation' is a direct result of SEEING and HEARING true knowledge."

"I once thought I knew what meditation was," I said. "Now, I'm not so sure."

"That's the problem. Because meditation has been so widely publicized, people think they know what it is. This has led people away from the truth instead of to it. Very few have any idea what the true state of meditation is.

"The state of meditation is reached when the mind has no thought from the past controlling it now. It is seeing, not from the outer, but from the inner. The true state of meditation is a divine conscious state.

"The true nature of mankind is to walk through life in this state. In a state of meditation one sees with clarity beyond the mind of mankind."

"And," I asked, "is it this state which brings true wisdom?"

"Yes. Wisdom is a state of consciousness. Each level of consciousness is a separate reality. Man is nothing but a conscious state suspended in time according to his state of evolution or level of consciousness.

"Intelligence," he continued, "is a state of mind, a belief."

"How then would you define true intelligence?" I asked.

Syd paused for a minute, looked up at the sky

which by now had become quite dark. He spoke quietly, under stars without number.

"True intelligence is a quiescent mind. It is a mind not held prisoner by thoughts which control you and make you see what-isn't instead of what-is."

He turned and began to walk slowly up the bank towards the house. Barb joined him and after a last look at the sea Bill and I followed.

There was nothing more to say. The lessons of life were infinite, like the sky that night, like the stars sprinkled across it. The man who walked before us had touched those stars and returned to us with their message.

CHAPTER 5

THE PATTERN OF LIFE

Early summer had come to our island. The days grew longer and the rains were now gentle and warm. A mantle of bright green covered the earth, dotted here and there with blossoms; yellow, pink and white. Fields everywhere were being plowed and gardens planted. The first really hot day brought with it memories of the beach, kids eating watermelon, of picnics and potato salad.

Time was passing in a way I could not remember. Bill and I were busy, building a new home and gardening and each evening brought amazement at what had been accomplished during the day. Yet life had never been so easy.

Each moment drifted into the next with little thought.

One morning I received a call from a man who identified himself briefly, saying that although I didn't know him he had heard much about Sydney Banks and those near him. He had heard good things, he went on; that many had found happiness through a method of teaching quite unique; that many had been healed of sickness and that our organization was a growing phenomenon he wished to investigate.

He added that he had a few days off and would

like to visit the island and speak with Syd. We agreed to meet the next morning at the ferry terminal and he thanked me profusely when I told him I would contact Syd and try to arrange a meeting.

Robert, my caller, was vague about his reasons for coming. Reasons, I knew, were meaningless for he would be placing himself in contact with the source of purest truth.

The next morning I recognized him immediately. He was wearing a business suit and carried a valise in one hand and an attaché case in the other.

On the way to Syd's he informed me that he had been involved in many awareness and spiritual groups. He had done research on still others and was thinking of beginning a group himself.

We drove slowly through the winding country-side and not once did he look at the incomparable vistas that lie on either side. His brow was furrowed and he talked continuously, though quite fluently of his intellectual accomplishments.

He appeared to be a deeply tormented man. The very mind of which he was so proud seemed to hold him in an intolerable grip.

"It sounds like you have been searching for something for quite a while," I finally said.

Robert looked at me in disbelief that I should say such a thing and hurriedly assured me that he was very happy, that he had already succeeded in the professional goals he had set for himself in life.

Once at Syd and Barb's with the introductions over, we all settled comfortably in the living room. Robert immediately unsnapped his briefcase and took out an imposing sheaf of typewritten papers and a few pamphlets.

"Here is my resume and some credentials I thought you'd like to see."

He placed them on the table in front of Syd.

Syd glanced at the enormous amount of papers and burst out laughing.

Our visitor literally bristled and said quite indignantly, "Well… aren't you going to read them?"

Still laughing, Syd answered, "I don't care who you are or what you have done in the past!"

"How can you possibly help me if you don't know who and what I am?" came an incredulous reply.

Syd turned slightly, laid his hand gently on Robert's shoulder and looked him straight in the eye. "But I already KNOW you!"

"That's impossible!" he sputtered in complete confusion. "How can you possibly know me? Why, we've never met before!"

Syd spoke, very slowly and distinctly: "Listen very carefully to what I have to say. Perhaps you will find what you are looking for…

"Mankind is energy manifest into form via a thought process. This thought process has a pattern and every living soul MUST conform to this pattern. There is a big pattern and a little pattern. If you SEE the big pattern you will see there is only one truth. The big cosmic thought is the only truth that exists. The little thought is truth to the mind. However, each mind being individualized, we live not in truth but in the illusion."

The mind of our guest had already raced ahead.

"How does this pattern, as you call it, work?"

"Just listen," Syd told him. "Just listen!"

It appeared this was something Robert seldom did. I had the feeling he had come, not to hear our views, but to expound at length on his own.

We sat in silence for a few minutes while Robert stared at the carpet. He then lifted his head, looked towards Syd and said, "Go ahead."

His brow was furrowed, and he was thinking so hard one could almost hear the wheels turning.

Syd looked as though he might grin, but instead began to speak.

"The pattern I speak of cannot be explained. It is far too complicated.

"The Allness is the big pattern and the Isness is the little pattern. The Isness is created from the Allness, therefore the Allness and the Isness are ONE. Here is where the secret to life lies. The trouble lies with the world trying to break the little pattern instead of the big cosmic one."

Syd paused and glanced around the room at our puzzled faces.

"Let me put it another way. There is an inside pattern and an outside pattern to life. Who you are and what you are is the outside pattern. On the other hand, the inside pattern is spiritual or cosmic. The spiritual or cosmic pattern is all that REALLY exists.

"Once you start to SEE how this inside pattern works, you step into another reality; the world within. Here is where you will find the knowledge you seek. Here is where one sees with simplicity how the mind works; within the boundaries of itself, thus seeing only in blindness and not SEEING at all."

Syd ran his fingers through his beard as if he were pondering, then continued.

"All life derives from a cosmic thought which is so pure there are no judgments. It is the mind of man that judges, analyzes, and breaks the pattern of understanding. When this occurs, the creation of desire, anger, jealousy and hate are manifest into form, creating our social and mental problems in life.

"Find your true identity and you will find love and understanding beyond your wildest imagination. If you find the source of the energy of all things you will surely find the secret to life and the mystery of the pattern you seek."

Robert's computer-like mind once again sprang into action.

"Where is this source you speak of?"

"The secret," continued Syd, "lies deep in the land of knowledge."

"How does one find this land?"

"This, my friend, takes courage. First, one must prepare oneself to SEE the golden chariot, then perhaps someday it will take you to your destination."

Syd told our visitor more of the golden chariot, of which he often spoke. Robert listened in silence, then appeared to become impatient.

"How far away is this 'Land of Knowledge?' " he asked, as though he did not believe such a place existed.

"A blink of an eye away," came the reply.

"Well, if everything is so simple, why don't I see it?"

"Because," said Syd, "you are lost in the confusion of life via your mind with all its beliefs."

This was simply too much! Robert became instantly angry, stood up and began to speak. He told us of the knowledge he had gained by years of intent study. He had read widely and spoke knowledgably of what he'd read. He did indeed have many profound truths, but I knew these were not his own, but simply borrowed statements.

He spoke of inner peace and self-realization, yet he himself held no peace. His face was desperately unhappy and as he spoke he clenched and unclenched his hands. He told of the security he had found by discovering exactly who and what he was.

He spoke of spiritual illumination while experiencing total insecurity. A few words had challenged all his beliefs and left him struggling to sustain a frightened ego.

Finally, after many long and painful minutes Robert sat, trembling and exhausted. He had tried valiantly to prove to himself that he, too, knew the secrets of life and he had failed.

Syd began again to speak, his voice so gentle I knew he felt nothing but compassion for this man.

"Knowledge," he said softly, "is NOT the memorization of words. True knowledge is an experience of this knowledge being a fact, an experience which must come from within yourself. When knowledge is put to the pen or spoken it no longer remains a fact but reverts back to a belief. This is why truth is hidden from the mind of man."

Robert's voice had subtly changed, losing some of its brash confidence.

"Are you saying that all the words of wisdom written and spoken throughout the ages have been in vain?"

"No, I am not saying that. Although the written and spoken words are converted back to beliefs, they may be used as a guide to help you find the fact, to help you find TRUE knowledge."

Syd rose from his chair, disappeared into the kitchen and was soon back with tea. He chatted with his visitor for a few minutes about the island and I could see Robert beginning to relax a little. We left shortly and at the door, Syd held out his hand and suggested, "Have a good time, Robert. Look around the island and just enjoy yourself."

"Thank you, I'd like to do that," came the reply.

We drove to a near-by resort where Robert would stay. I asked if he would like to join Bill and I for dinner but he declined politely and added, "I've got a lot to think about!"

CHAPTER 6

THE GREAT COSMIC FACT

I awoke the next morning to find sun streaming through the window and knew it would be another glorious day. By 10 a.m. I had picked up our visitor and once again we headed for Syd and Barb's. If anything, Robert looked worse this morning. He mentioned that he hadn't slept very well and I envisioned him lying awake 'til the wee small hours with the wheels grinding away in his over-active brain.

"I find Syd a very interesting man," he said.

"It's clear he's had some kind of illumination experience. However, he isn't saying anything new. I'm quite familiar with his ideas, although I must say his manner of presentation is unique."

"These are not ideas!" I replied. "You can be sure if Syd is speaking of something, he is speaking fact!" and I then related my own experience, the moment I'd discovered the difference between belief and fact.

Long ago I'd spoken to Syd about a problem I'd had. Syd responded with a few short words, but I felt I had heard those same words many times. I became impatient, and said, "I already know that!" but quick as a flash he replied, "You THINK you know it!"

In one amazing moment of clarity I had discovered the difference between knowing and thinking you know; the difference between belief and fact. It was obvious if I'd known the truth behind Syd's words, the problem itself would never have existed.

Robert did not comment. I knew he still believed the spiritual information he'd gathered to be truly his, although in fact, it had brought no results.

Minutes later Syd and Barb greeted us at the door and suggested we stay outside and enjoy the sunshine. Although the sun was warm, the grass was still damp with dew. We gathered lawn chairs and sat quietly for a moment, then Robert began to speak.

"I know you are trying to tell me something, Syd. I feel here a quality I've never experienced before. You all have a radiance about you, an intense feeling of life. But I can't figure out what exactly it is."

"The trouble is, Robert, that you talk to yourself constantly and never give yourself an opportunity to see anything new! You see, there are two realities. One is the reality you now live in and the other lies deep within. Both of these realities are a fact!

"The difference comes when you realize that one reality is a mind fact and the other reality is a cosmic or spiritual fact. All things derive from this cosmic fact via a super-conscious state. This super-conscious state lies within every living person on earth. This is where you will find happiness and the secret of life.

"The difficulty lies with the mind trying to figure out how the cosmic world works. When you begin to see with clarity, you will see both realities as perfect. You will realize that two plus two in the outside reality do not make four in the inside reality.

"If you SEE this as a fact, you will at that moment begin to find the secret of the Missing Link. You will begin to see what-is instead of what-isn't. What-is is the perfection of life in motion. What-isn't is the mind seeing the imperfections of life, therefore creating an imperfect world.

"Remember my dear friend, it is a world of thought! The thought is the cause and the effect is the result of the thought. Think negatively and the manifestation of the thought will create a negative life. Think positively and the world you now know will turn to beauty."

Robert nodded in agreement with this last statement.

"I once read…" he began, but his voice trailed off into nothing. Perhaps he was beginning to see!

Syd continued, "Everyone looks for information to reach higher states of consciousness. This is a pit-fall of the mind. On the contrary, all you have to do is raise your level of consciousness. Then the already KNOWN appears. You will then see more of what-is and what-isn't begins to fade away, truth being the victor!"

With this, Syd jumped to his feet and gaily announced, "Let's have lunch!"

For the first time I saw a big smile on Robert's face and what a difference it made! He appeared more relaxed than I had seen him and was genuinely enjoying himself. We all helped to prepare sandwiches and took them back outside. We ate, laughed and joked. Robert displayed a quick wit and joined in the hilarity with enthusiasm.

After lunch he told Syd there was a question he'd like to ask. "Go right ahead," Syd replied.

Robert hesitated, then finally came out with it, as if the question embarrassed him, "What about love?"

I couldn't help but smile. Robert was so worldly-wise and dignified yet so totally innocent one couldn't help but feel affection for him.

Syd did not seem to notice his discomfort and promptly replied: "Love and understanding are the principles by which all things are created here on earth. When you lose this love and understanding, YOU are lost!

"This creates confusion in your life which leads to stress, strain and boredom. These in turn lead to still more serious problems. To find love and understanding one must look WITHIN ONESELF. Here lie the treasures of life in abundance.

"To study other people's beliefs, concepts, etc., is really of very little value. All one learns is another set of beliefs with which to judge and analyze, adding yet more confusion to an already confused mind. Look WITHIN YOURSELF! Then you will begin to see the true reality of life. This is how you will find your long-lost love and understanding!"

With the sheer power of the truth of Syd's words, unceasingly he told us, "go within, go within!"

For those who did awaited the treasures of which he spoke. However, at the mere mention of a confused mind, Robert's ego had once again taken control and he changed visibly.

"What do you mean, go within?" he demanded. "Where else could one be but inside oneself?"

"Believe me," replied Syd, "when your level of consciousness rises you will know what is meant by 'inside.' Like all truth, it is unexplainable. All you have to do is listen."

Robert stood up quickly and I could see the talk of love and understanding was very dangerous territory for him.

"I'd like to listen," he said, "I really would! Unfortunately, I have an appointment tomorrow and have to get back to the city. I've enjoyed our discussions and perhaps we can exchange views again some other time."

He thanked Syd and Barb for their hospitality and walked briskly towards the car. We returned to the resort for his luggage and then headed towards the ferry. Robert was very quiet during the drive and spoke again only when we had reached our destination.

"I'm glad you've found what you are looking for," he said, "but for me, Syd's doctrine is too simplistic."

I knew exactly what he meant. Like him, I and many others had once disbelieved the simplicity of truth. With a feeling of warmth in my heart, I replied,

"Robert, it is beyond the imagination! One must walk in the way to experience how easy it is, how easy it makes life."

I recalled words Syd had written some time before, which I had read and reread, "Once having accepted the power of truth, having surrendered to this power, there is no longer a necessity for taking thought for the how's and whys of one's life.

"From this moment on, truth will guide and protect. From this moment, we need only walk with ease and beauty throughout our days, knowing we have found the way."

We said good-bye and Robert walked towards the ticket booth. He looked old and tired, scurrying off to his next encounter. I knew he must be weary of the constant search. The laws of the universe work equally well for everyone and Robert was no exception.

Although he possessed a brilliant mind he was simply not ready to hear truth. I felt that for a moment he had caught a glimpse of a new reality. Perhaps someday he would be back, perhaps not. "Good luck!" I called, and he turned and waved.

What a contrast his life was from my own. I felt not judgment but deep understanding, for I had once lived a life lost in thought. I felt so strongly the touch and power of truth in my life.

At such times, I know I have discovered The Way and that I am walking in it. I feel such faith as I have never known, for I am surrounded and protected by truth. If a thought should appear that I do not want, truth hastens to show it for its worthlessness.

At every moment it is here to show the way I must live.

To spend one brief moment in the joy and glory of this way is to know beyond belief there can be no other.

CHAPTER 7

THE SHADOW OF A DREAM

Several days had passed since Robert wandered in and out of my life and something of his visit lingered on. It was not he, the person, who occupied my thoughts but rather his mind that fascinated me.

I had experienced with a new clarity the power of mind to keep us locked in the illusion. I had seen Robert's mind fencing with truth, darting here and there, never resting for a moment lest truth should gain entry.

He had asked questions, the same questions I had once asked. I had seen the unbelievable cleverness of his intellect disguise the answers to conform with his belief system. Thus I had seen more of myself, of my own mind and how it worked. I had experienced mind at play; its amazing agility and its ability to hide truth.

The nature of thought has ever been a mystery to mankind and to have even a glimmer at its inner meaning filled me with excitement. There is a joy that comes inevitably when mind opens itself to something new and sees something never seen before. I felt like I had a new toy and wanted to share it.

I called Syd, wishing to convey something of what I felt. Immediately, he sensed my meaning and said, "The mind is a wonderful thing: It is the instrument by which mankind receives and projects life."

We talked then for a few minutes of mind, of the two different worlds and Syd continued: "If this same mind is contaminated with ignorance, it becomes jammed. It does not receive or send facts, only the self-created beliefs which lead man astray."

"And," I said, now excited to be 'getting' it, "we all contaminate our minds in a different way according to our own beliefs!"

"Right!" Syd exclaimed. "As spiritual beings we all play the same identical game as every other being on earth. What we APPEAR to be in this life is our own personal disguise. Penetrate the illusion of this disguise and you will discover the pattern of life and the treasures that lie within!

"The way to penetrate this disguise is to ignore it. Talk from within! Live from within. Here we are all truly one conscious state. Here, we can all understand each other and live in harmony, for here there is only ONE TRUTH!"

"ONE TRUTH!" After we'd hung up, the words returned again and again to my consciousness. I was seeing them in a new light.

Bill returned from work and over dinner we talked of the 'one truth.'

"I've been thinking about it all afternoon," I said. "There are as many disguises as there are people on earth. Each disguise has its own set of problems.

"There are groups, or committees, that specialize in the problems of children, of slow learners, of the physically handicapped. There are groups for the emotionally disturbed, for marital and sexual problems. Some groups investigate the crises of middle age and others try to help older people adjust to retirement. There are groups trying to solve the problems of each disguise. We've used our minds to make life appear so incredibly complicated!"

"Yet how beautiful it is, that all problems disappear when truth is heard, the one great truth," replied Bill. "We would all live in heaven here on earth if our minds could accept this simple fact."

We were to learn more of the one truth. The next morning Bill and I went to Ganges to browse around the Farmer's Market. The atmosphere was gay with movement and color, with many familiar faces.

After an hour or so, we withdrew for a quiet moment to the little park nearby. We found a bench and watched as a boat occasionally docked, or one left the harbour. The day was warm and fine, and behind us, children squealed with delight on the slide and swings.

A couple walked towards us wearing bright summer clothing, their faces tanned and smiling.

"Oh, no!" said Syd as they drew near. "I was just saying to Barb, I hope we don't run into you two today!"

But his friendly grin gave him away and we laughed and made room for them on the bench. Soon

I remembered the 'One Truth' and told Syd of the conversation Bill and I'd had.

Syd smiled and said, "You see, if your mind disbelieves there is only one truth, then you will create other beliefs and call them your truth. This again is life in perfect motion, using free will and free mind to see whatever you wish to see.

"You are then obviously not using your greatest gift. Therefore, you must try and figure out life.

"It is the mind which creates the division between what you see and what REALLY exists. This division is known as yin and yang, good and evil, top and bottom, heaven and earth."

"How does top and bottom fit in?" I asked.

Syd grinned. "We'll get to that later!"

"Now, the higher your conscious state rises, the less this division exists. The reason for this is that each level brings forth the necessary knowledge which helps you SEE the illusion of opposites. It helps you to SEE the oneness of all things."

Syd was grinning like a Cheshire cat. I had asked about 'one truth' and he had replied with opposites! He seemed to go from "A" to "C" without going through "B". And whenever he spoke of nothingness, I was lost. I told him so and again he laughed.

"Now listen," he said quite seriously. Syd paused as if to make sure we were listening very carefully. "True knowledge is the missing link between the ALLNESS and the ISNESS! This ISNESS is created from the ALLNESS of ALL things!"

"Syd!" I exclaimed. "You know we can't possibly understand that!"

"Then why don't you stop trying?" came the instant reply.

The directness of his question startled me. "Of course," I thought! "How simple!"

Yet my mind was whispering in my ear... "How will I ever get it if I don't think about it?"

Syd's next words were perfect.

"If you seek via your own silly little beliefs, you will never SEE or HEAR! You will hear only the echoes of your own mind."

Once again, he seemed to read my very thoughts. I had to admit I was hearing only echoes and they were certainly of no help.

"It is SEEING this isness," Syd continued, "and accepting it as a fact that leads to knowing. Now, each time you SEE a fact you begin to see with greater clarity. This breaks down the negative side of life you now see and helps you SEE the isness."

The echoes returned. "Now I'm more confused than ever!"

"You are STILL trying to figure it out. Haven't I told you many times, one cannot possibly HEAR or SEE truth via the thinking process of the mind?

"Just listen! Listen without thought! I spoke to you long ago of no-thought.

"This beautiful state is the state of meditation. It is in this conscious state that one SEES with crystal clarity.

"You see, it is very difficult to believe that the what-is and the isness from the MIND of mankind is an illusion, therefore man sees what-isn't. When you begin to see this as a fact, life changes because you see the fallacy and drama of life. It makes one realize that life is truly the shadow of a dream and always will be, with no end and no beginning. It just is!"

We sat in a stillness inspired by these magic words.

Syd spoke then and asked, "Do you remember when we first met? You both believed that to receive knowledge all one had to do was memorize the WORDS! After you had memorized them, you thought you knew for a FACT what they meant.

"It was not fact, but merely belief. Once again your chariot was made of tinsel and thread and led you only to more confusion. However, your courage to encounter these false chariots had led to what you now SEE!"

He paused then and looked at Bill and I with that twinkle. "I admit at times I felt like giving you both up as a bad dream!"

We laughed together in knowing memory of those days.

"You see, my friends, there is no knowledge in the world. There is only the belief that the knowledge exists. One must go beyond the word to the experience, the experience of SEEING knowledge sprinkled upon your belief to change it to a living fact.

"Wisdom is the divine instrument which is used to open the doors to what all mankind seeks. Wisdom and true knowledge are the same. Wisdom, like knowledge, prepares you for the golden chariot which will take you home to the land of knowledge.

"Here lies the center of all thought where the unexplainable is explained via simplicity. Here lies the Pearl of all Pearls. Here, my dear, dear friend, lies the secret of life!"

With Syd's last words, joy filled my heart. For perhaps someday, I too, would find the 'Pearl of Pearls.'

CHAPTER 8

THE RIDDLE OF DUALITY

The mystique of Salt Spring Island continued in its quiet and powerful way to draw those who would discover its secrets. For many came an immediate acceptance that the mysteries of mind would here be revealed. One such man, a psychologist, was to return again and again to our island.

We first met Roger Mills at a gathering one evening where Syd had spoken of the relationship between psychology and religion. Roger was clearly fascinated and later talked with Syd until it was time to leave.

The next day we were invited, along with Roger and a few others to visit with Syd and Barb. Because of ever growing demands upon Syd's time, few were now able to meet with him personally and we felt increasingly grateful for each hour we were able to spend in his presence. We arrived the next afternoon to find Syd and Roger already deep in conversation.

"Syd, I'm puzzled by what you're saying. Not a word of it is anything like what I heard last night."

"Roger, it is via the WORD that you will find the way. Yet it is via this same word that the way is lost. Therefore, the word is of no value. That is why you must go BEYOND the word to find the missing link."

"Missing Link?" laughed Roger...."now you sound like an anthropologist!"

"Not exactly," grinned Syd. "Not exactly!"

Roger smiled and his face crinkled up like a child's. I saw in him an openness, a genuine eagerness for more.

"SEEING," Syd continued, "is the stepping stone which leads to the missing link. This missing link is the one answer you seek. It is the missing link which turns belief into fact and guides you through life perfectly.

"The missing link is finding the NOTHINGNESS, dead center, between top and bottom. When you find this nothingness, you've found the ONENESS, which is the ALLNESS! Thus you realize the Isness is only a shadow of the Allness."

Roger looked confounded and shook his head. "I knew this was going to be interesting! Frankly Syd, I don't understand what you're saying."

We assured him that we didn't understand it either, that intellectual understanding of truth was unnecessary as well as totally impossible. Roger seemed to accept this and listened carefully as Syd went on.

"Truth cannot be understood by the mind, just as SEEING and HEARING cannot be explained. One can only guide, via the word. You alone must discover what SEEING and HEARING really are. Seeing and hearing as processes of the mind have their own limitations.

"On the other hand, SEEING and HEARING is the true process of life being manifest to show the fallacy of the illusion by revealing the true reality of life. It unveils the secret to mankind's true identity. It reveals the workings of the mind and its relationship to all our problems.

"The status quo of the mind of mankind is the creator of all our problems. When the mind tries to fix this self-created mess, it cannot, due to the fact mankind has not evolved enough. Here is where the mystery lies." Syd paused for a moment, looked around at all our earnest faces, then went on.

"To fix the unfixable, you must change the status quo of the mind by raising the conscious state. This is done, not intellectually by gathering details, but by SEEING and HEARING wisdom. You see, there is nothing gained in having more intellectual intelligence if it is not accompanied by the wisdom to use it properly."

A silence followed. Roger looked quite perplexed. I knew he was thinking, as I myself had done so often upon hearing these same words. I could almost predict his next question.

"There's seeing and there's ...SEEING, right! What's the difference?"

Syd glanced toward the window and something there captured and held him for long moments until I thought he wasn't going to answer, or else had completely forgotten about SEEING. One never knew!

"See that tree?" He nodded towards a towering cedar whose lower branches almost swept the ground beneath.

"Yesss…"Roger replied hesitantly, as if by now he weren't quite sure of anything.

"Everyone," continued Syd, "sees this same tree. Yet, a man of knowledge sees two trees. One is the illusion. The other is real!"

"Are you saying there are two trees?!!" Roger's voice was incredulous. "Are you seeing double?"

He glanced quickly out the window as if to make certain of the number of trees really there.

"No," Syd replied with a patient smile, "it has nothing to do with seeing double."

He paused. I knew that look! Syd was going to mystify us completely with a description of SEEING, one that none of us would SEE!"

Suddenly, he became very serious. "Listen!" His voice became a whisper… "but don't try to figure it out!"

Again, the voice changed. "The reason a man of knowledge SEES two trees is because they are one!

"You see two trees because they are one!" Roger was bewildered and his eyes swept around the room to each face, only to find we all looked as bewildered as he.

Syd was grinning and looked as if he might burst into great peals of laughter any moment. He knew he had us baffled!

"This can only be understood when you see IT in action," he continued. "IT being the essence of all life. To see IT needs no thought. IT is before the creation of the tree. IT just is! See life as just-is and you will see the duality from the singular is the creator of the illusionary duality. Therefore, there is no duality! Just IT!"

"Syd!" Roger exclaimed, "That's the most confusing sentence I've ever heard. You're talking in riddles!"

"Perhaps if you would just listen instead of trying to figure it out, you would see that it was YOU who created the riddle, not I!"

"I created the riddle?" came a disbelieving reply.

"Truth is not a riddle," Syd replied. "It is a simple fact. Not your fact – because your facts are of no value. They are only beliefs in the disguise of FACT.

"It is a riddle to you because your mind sees only one tree; therefore you are seeing in duality. If you could SEE the oneness, you would SEE two trees because the inside and the outside would exist at once, hence; two trees. Unless you SEE this you live in a world of duality, not ONENESS."

The look on Roger's face was priceless! I smiled. He was having his first experience with a man of knowledge. Syd was a master of disguise. In one afternoon he had been a psychologist; sophisticated, articulate and composed. Suddenly, he became a very wise-looking, bearded man, speaking gently of truth, of oneness.

Then, in a flash, he changed again. He grinned and gesticulated, became a trickster and spoke in riddles. Then a mystic, speaking in a hushed voice of SEEING. Next, an awareness teacher, or spiritual guide. In turn, Syd instantly became every ideal we might have of 'one who knew'.

The previous hour had left me speechless and I knew for Roger it must have been unforgettable. He stood and walked over to the sofa where Syd lounged in a state of great relaxation.

"Syd," he said, "you've taken the world apart, separated the pieces, and put them back together in a totally nonsensical order! You've threatened every belief I've ever had about life, about who and what I am!"

Roger sat again, and began to speak quietly. "But I love it! I love what you're saying. For years I've felt a great responsibility towards my patients and students. I've always felt they looked to me for a wisdom I didn't possess. It's been a struggle to maintain that image. I feel for the first time, I've met a greater wisdom. Real wisdom."

He looked towards Syd with a look of admiration, of deepest respect and said simply, "Thank you."

CHAPTER 9

THE ORIGINAL MIND

Time passed, each day moving through our lives, each bringing with it something new. Syd often spoke of the unreality of time and we were beginning to have a hint of his meaning.

We began to measure our days not by hours and minutes, but by feelings, by experiences.

Lifetimes could pass in a single week, for in such time we might leave behind years of past; forgotten and unneeded. An hour could stretch to encompass many levels of consciousness, many different realities. We learned to move very softly though life, to let life weave itself through us.

One evening after dinner Bill and I strolled through the fragrance and delight of our garden. We noted with pleasure the health and vigor of the vegetables, the luxuriant masses of flowers. Pausing, we looked out over the hills. The sky was purple and orange as the sun dipped into the sea in a spectacular finale. I noticed for the first time that the days had grown shorter.

Just then I felt the evening breeze and it held a hint of coolness. A few leaves from a nearby tree were caught in a small gust and drifted to the ground nearby. Suddenly I knew summer was over, even though there would still be a few days at the beach, a few more picnics.

Autumn was in the air, and the remembrance of fall on Salt Spring Island brought a tremendous feeling of well-being, of thanksgiving. Soon the maples would be a fiery blaze and the apples red and heavy on the branches.

We stood quietly in the gathering darkness and gazed lovingly towards the home we had just built together. We had moved only recently, and the new house stands only feet from the canal where the quiet waters had always drawn us. It is a magical place, and the tide's ebb and flow reflects our lives with a gliding tranquility.

Slowly the headlights of a car rounded the top of the hill and we walked to meet it as it turned into our driveway. It was Roger, but definitely not the Roger we had met such a short time ago. He came towards us, and his walk was freer, his face softer. In his eyes we saw a glow, a spark that had not been there before. We knew he, too, had been touched by truth.

Roger would be leaving the next day and we had decided to gather for a little 'farewell.' As we waited for the others we spoke with Roger about his visit.

Through his eyes we saw again the uniqueness of our lives here on Salt Spring. He openly and honestly shared with us what he'd seen, felt and experienced since coming to the island.

Roger's first impressions confirmed his feeling that indeed something special was happening on Salt

Spring. Upon arrival he'd met a couple who'd been listening to Syd for some time.

"They had a certain look about them," he said, "as if they knew something." As he spoke with them Roger began to realize they had a knowledge of life he did not possess that seemed to go beyond his academic knowledge. He had been doing research on belief systems, he told us, and had spent many years in the Far East studying.

"I learned they had totally different belief systems than we in the West. But they were still controlled by their beliefs. Here, for the first time, I met people living 'beyond beliefs.'" The effect on Roger had been instantaneous.

"I felt an immediate sense of dropping a lot of groundless insecurities. I didn't know why, didn't understand it, but I knew that speaking with these people had changed my life. Then, I met Syd," he continued, "and with his first words I realized he Knew."

Syd and Barb soon arrived and we settled comfortably before the fire. I felt Roger was indeed an exceptional man and recalled aloud something Syd had told us long ago.

"Many will come," he had said, "but few will listen! Their egos will not allow them to hear." How prophetic those words!

"The mind cannot possibly comprehend the Allness," Syd began. "The mind lives in its own little individualized, illusionary world attached to what is called ego. The ego is the stumbling block to showing you what you seek. It is a matter of self-importance and the creator of all our problems."

"Then the mind is of no value?" asked Roger.

"On the contrary," Syd replied. "It is your most valuable instrument. One could say it is your world. But you must learn how to take care of it and keep it clean. It is the clean mind that enables the eyes to SEE!

"Do you remember we spoke of the pattern of life?"

Roger nodded and Syd continued.

"When the mind transcends itself to the big pattern, wisdom appears. From this inner pattern one SEES with clarity the simplicity of thought and its relationship to life. This is impossible to comprehend from the mind, so it is sometimes called religion, sometimes philosophy. Either way it is perfect psychology, and perfect psychiatry when HEARD!

"You see, all paths are a guide to finding IT. Each path is a small part of IT. The paradox is, you must give up the small part to find IT. Otherwise there is a missing link between you and IT, IT being the essence of all things."

Roger looked thoughtful. "Truth seems to cover all things," he said, "I've always felt the psychological and the spiritual to be worlds apart."

"Perhaps I should explain what is meant by 'spiritual,'" Syd continued. "All life is spiritual because all life is an illusion. When the illusion is in form, we call it life and it is quite tangible to the mind. Here in the illusion, knowledge from the mind is something we can pass on to each other under the name of a belief or a concept, 'intellectual intelligence.'

"A fact is spiritual, because it is BEFORE the mind of mankind. Only to the HEARER does it make sense. Here the fallacy of trying to solve your problems by intellectual methods appears as it really is, a cosmic joke."

Roger spoke up with great confidence and security in his voice, "I want to find the knowledge you speak of!"

"INSIDE." Very quietly, Syd replied. "Inside lies the abundance of knowledge you seek."

"Inside," reflected Roger. "Syd, it sounds... well, selfish somehow. I want to help those less fortunate than myself."

"First," said Syd, "you must go INSIDE! Find your true identity. Only then can you help others. Otherwise, it is only the blind leading the blind."

His words were powerful, and had the same effect on Roger. They seemed to leave him more relaxed, as though he had surrendered something deep within and had a glimpse of INSIDE.

"You see, Roger, INSIDE is just an expression. It helps you to realize that somewhere in your super-conscious state you hold the secret which all mankind seeks."

Syd paused, and into his eyes came a look from far away. "One could say INSIDE is that part of your consciousness that at the present moment is unknown to you. It is SEEING beyond what your mind has computed.

"The memorization of wisdom turns it into an intellectual belief or concept, whereas true wisdom is a direct experience of contacting the original mind that lies within. Your mind does not hold the secret to realizing what INSIDE means. You do not know of its existence, therefore no one can tell you or anyone else.

"One must find it for oneself. Once you find it the knowledge you seek will come. Here is where the original mind knows its original identity." Syd became silent, as if exploring the depths of 'The Original Mind.' We waited, for we knew he would take us with him on his explorations.

"Take the electric light bulb, for instance," he began. "When the original thought of such a thing occurred, you can be sure it was not a 'little-mind' thought, but a direct insight from original mind. It had nothing to do with intellect! It was wisdom coming to light!"

Oh, the wondrous way Syd perceived the world! To him, a mere light bulb became "Wisdom, coming to light!" How beautiful were his words, how tempting, how they led us on and on towards ever more wisdom.

"The science of the inner mind," he continued, "is religion. It is the divulging of the super-consciousness that lies within. When this knowledge is divulged, it is not from your mind or my mind, but from the ORIGINAL MIND.

"The ORIGINAL MIND is before the creation of the ego and is neutral in thought. It is the original mind of all mankind.

"This is why there is only ONE TRUTH, for there is only ONE ORIGINAL MIND!"

Again, a gentle quietness descended upon the room. We watched the moon, full and white, drifting through the sky. It hesitated a moment, lighting a shimmery trail across the water, then moved on.

All evening the fire had roared and crackled to accompany our talk and laughter. Now only glowing embers remained to accompany our stillness. Soft flickers of light danced along the walls.

The room, the house, the very earth seems to sigh dreamily along with us, prepared for night. Tomorrow is a long thought away and only a timeless moment remains, a moment we share together. Peace steals into the room, softly at first, then alive and glowing like the embers.

Peace; a feeling so intense I realize I have never known it before. A feeling rich with love and being loved, of being held safely in the arms of life. The feeling comes from deep within, from a place never known before but always there. The feeling is mine now, and I know it will always be.

CHAPTER 10

THE MISSING LINK

Inviting, mysterious and ever-changing, Salt Spring is indeed an Island of magic. Yet it is not really magic; we have simply discovered the right use of the mind. Here to guide us we find one amongst us who has touched depths of understanding we can only observe with wonder and probably never really know; philosopher and teacher Sydney Banks.

We spend long evenings now before the fire to absorb; to assimilate the powerful experiences we have had, to incorporate their lessons more fully into our daily lives. It has been a time of great learning. Changes now seem less dramatic, more subtle, as we begin to touch realms of existence deep within.

We've learned patience; to take each moment of the day, to savour it, to enjoy the completeness of its unique fulfillment. We've learned not to grasp at life, but to wait patiently for life to reveal its treasures, each in its special time and place. And we have been richly rewarded for our patience.

We've learned, too, of gratitude; that each desire for more only brings less, for then we see not what we have, but what we would have. We've begun to see that a bounteous abundance of all the good things of life has been freely given us and we must only accept and give thanks for that which is already ours.

We've learned of feelings, for Syd has taught us that we must express the wondrous new deep feelings we have discovered or our spiritual knowledge becomes useless, and our words just words. Our knowledge comes alive only as we leave the world of thought, our analytical and habitual thinking behind and express those feelings from deep within our soul.

We've learned of words, magic words. With words, we share our hopes, our experiences, and our feelings, and with words we touch one another and are touched by truth. Words of truth are the most beautiful, for they lead us within, they move our hearts and stir our souls with their breathtaking simplicity.

With the coming of winter, one could feel not only the changing weather and the end of summer, but also the end of something much more vast and deep; something almost indescribable. The most amazing experience of my life felt as if it were coming to an end.

Dr. Roger Mills soon moved to Salt Spring Island, and my most distinct memory is a dinner at Roger's where he brewed dark roast coffee for us, using real coffee beans, a grinder and a French press. This was an unusual treat as we had become accustomed to our ritual of herbal tea. Fresh from the city, he brought with him more sophisticated ways and we welcomed him as a close friend.

Soon, he was joined by George Pransky and other visitors from the helping professions; psychologists, mental health professionals and therapists who had heard of Sydney Banks and his teachings and their profound effect on those seeking help with the problems of life.

For many years, I had spent much of my time with Syd, working on our books; editing, revising, and always listening, listening as amazing new and fresh ideas and inspirations poured forth. I had travelled to other islands, and cities with Syd as he began to be invited farther afield as his reputation as a healer and teacher grew. I would share my story and the book, *Island of Knowledge* that we had written together. Now Syd was being called forth to a new adventure. The wider world had discovered the magic of Sydney Banks and demanded his attention.

Our book was drawing to a close, as was our time together. It was time for me also to take my newfound knowledge and freedom and move on. Syd and I met less and less often as he began to travel and the greater commitments of a world teacher took up more of his time.

Yet the old magic still continued on occasion, and now I felt how incredible had been my journey and friendship with Syd, and how fortunate I had been to spend days each week with him, the two of us sitting at his kitchen table, or mine, as streams of consciousness revealed deeper and more amazing secrets.

One day, he called excitedly and was soon knocking at my door with two sheets of paper in his hand. Another breakthrough had come, and he wished to savour and digest its significance, and wished it to be part of the book. This inspiration too, was truly Beyond Beliefs. "It's The Missing Link," he repeated several times.

We sat down together over tea for what would be our last working session on the book.

"It's The Missing Link," he kept repeating.

"All paths are a guide to finding IT, each path is a small part of IT. The paradox is, you must give up the small part to find IT, otherwise there is a Missing Link between you and IT, IT being the essence of all things."

As Syd read from his notes, I saw he had underlined IT, and as he spoke, I knew he had had another realization at a higher, deeper level and it seemed a whole new world had opened up to him as we spoke. I had never seen Syd, usually so calm and quiet, in such a state of excitement. In my bewilderment, I asked questions, but he just put them aside as he continued.

"As you start to find this Missing Link, evolution takes place and unfolds the mystery of life."

I couldn't resist, "but what has evolution got to do with psychology?"

"The evolution of man is not time as you think it is," he replied. "On the contrary, it is the evolution of the conscious state that lies within. The world slows down, and gives you a chance to SEE another reality."

Amazingly, at that moment, I knew I *had* seen another reality. Those sessions with Syd as we worked, those evenings with Syd and Barb and our small group before the fire, the public talks and then the excitement as the larger world had discovered Sydney Banks, the philosopher and mystic, all had been part of another reality for myself, and for many others.

I had seen another reality, and as friend, teacher, philosopher and mystic Sydney Banks had promised, it had all been Beyond Belief. Later that evening, after an unforgettable day, I recalled an evening several weeks before and what I had written at that time:

Slowly the last rays of the sun are reflected on the still waters and we turn again towards the fire. Seated in its glow Syd speaks, "Inside," he says quietly. "Inside lies the abundance of knowledge you seek."

It is a moment I will never forget.

END

CPSIA information can be obtained
at www.ICGtesting.com
Printed in the USA
LVOW03s2158200917
549254LV00001B/4/P